THE  TIMES BOOK OF

CHURCH
CATS

Also available from HarperCollins*Publishers* by Richard Surman:

Cathedral Cats
Castle Cats

THE TIMES BOOK OF
CHURCH
CATS

Richard Surman

with drawings by Peter Arscott

HarperCollins*Publishers*

HarperCollins*Publishers*
77–85 Fulham Palace Road, London W6 8JB
www.**fire**and**water**.com

First published in Great Britain in 1999 by
HarperCollins*Publishers*
This edition 2000

3 5 7 9 10 8 6 4

A catalogue record for this book
is available from the British Library.

ISBN 0 00 628125 7

Printed and bound in Hong Kong

Contents

THE TIMES BOOK OF

CHURCH

CATS

Introduction

Of all the cats that I have tried to trace in particular places, church cats are the most elusive. I had imagined a class of cat that strolled gently between a homely parish church and a warm rectory hearth. What I had not taken into consideration is the sad fact that many churches are underused, and don't have resident vicars, let alone cats. Many of the clerics that I initially contacted were dog-owners, to whom the mention of a cat was anathema. The research began to resemble an investigation.

But gradually stories emerged about cats and churches; the first successful contact was on my own doorstep. It became clear that church cats are a remarkably varied lot – a mixture of strays, sentinels, invaders and official residents. Ledbury's church cats, Flossie and Corrie, secured their hold on the church by preventing dogs from entering the churchyard. Korky had lived in a tree for months before being housed by the vicar and his family. Cheeky, who roamed the garden of St Wulfram's rectory for six months, had to resort to breaking and entering in order to win residential rights, whilst Brecon's Buonaventura was a disaster-causing gift. At the other end of the scale are Tano, a patrician tabby point

Siamese at Malmesbury Abbey, and the gentle Minou, who haunts the city rooftops of St Mary-le-Bow.

Cats have always played a large part in my life. As a child my family had a succession of characterful cats, and I have striven hard to maintain the tradition: the latest additions to the Surman household are two chocolate brown Burmese sisters, who utterly dominate domestic routine. Curious to a fault, there is not a corner of our house that escapes their attention: the cellar, airing cupboards, bookshelves, the shower, kitchen cupboards, drawers, fire-places, wardrobes and beds – the cats always appear in the most unexpected places. But what good company they are (and this is a joy that only those who appreciate cats can understand)! Friendly, talkative, affectionate, unpredictable, sometimes plain crazy, and always independent – what more could one want in an animal companion?

Photographing cats away from the studio is always fraught. I often wish that they were a little less independent and unpredictable. The techniques for taking pictures of cats in their surroundings are patience, a willingness to stalk and an unending supply of cat treats. Be prepared and quick. If you have to stop and load film, the cat may well have moved on, and once the cat's attention is lost, you've had it. Anticipate the territory and likely movements of a cat. I often try to be in position in advance of a cat moving from one place to another. On the purely technical side a camera with automatic exposure facilities helps, although the settings have to be overridden in any situation of strong backlight. I use a tripod too, especially when trying to take a shot of a cat in repose in very low light. But beware: some cats take fright at the sight of a tripod, so a small beanbag can be used to rest the camera on. Don't loom over a cat that doesn't know you. They find it threatening. A trail of tasty morsels can encourage a cat to stay in one particular place. Bits of string are useful for catching a cat's attention. But the most important technique is to be gentle, and to have a real affection for your subject.

Many thanks to Elspeth Taylor and James Catford at HarperCollins for their support and encouragement with *Church Cats*, and to Peter Arscott for providing such excellent illustrations of the various featured churches. I am grateful for the help given by the many people who did not have cats, but gave me further clues as to where to search.

I am also very grateful to Brother Aidan and the friars of Hilfield Friary, and to Brother Joseph OSB and the Benedictine community at Buckfast Abbey, for their kind and welcoming hospitality.

Finally I would like to thank my wife Blanca for her patience and my young sons Carlos and Gabriel, who took a keen interest in the book, and with whom I discussed at length the various attributes of this latest miscellany of cats.

ALL SAINTS', WEST HAM

Sylvester

As befits a cat who lives in one of the tougher areas of East London, Sylvester has a turn of speed that outruns any possible source of trouble.

When I visited Sylvester he was not in the most receptive of moods. Julian Scharf had just returned from several weeks in India; West Ham had just lost a match. Sylvester was taking every opportunity to express his disgust at his team having lost and being left behind, and was stalking about in high dudgeon. The arrival of someone with a camera was the last straw, even if they were offering edible bribes for one to hold one's position for just a few seconds.

The Rev. Dr Julian Scharf has spent many years of ministry in London. Before moving with his family to West Ham, he had been in Stepney, at St Paul's, Shadwell, where they had two cats, Andrew and Dennis. The latter cat had been discovered, under an old wig in the church dustbin, by the organist. Part-Siamese Andrew was not impressed with the new arrival, and made his reproachful contribution to church music by sitting on one particular gravestone and howling during choir practice.

Sylvester lives a little way from the Church of All Saints, West Ham, so his contact with church life is based mainly around meetings and groups that gather in the vicarage, where he spends a good part of the day sitting in Julian Scharf's in-tray. Extracting the day's mail can be time consuming. Not liking to disturb Sylvester's repose, Julian Scharf resorts to wiggling the mail out from underneath him. The feel of

Pigeon spotting.

movement under Sylvester triggers a response well known to those who have much to do with cats; a subtle shift whereby a cat changes its mass, seeming to double its weight and appear lifeless at the same time.

Sylvester loves the outdoor life, exploring his neighbours' gardens as well as his own. The sound of fluttering wings doesn't signify to Sylvester an angelic vision, but rather the final approach of a hapless pigeon shortly to have a rather closer experience of the hereafter. Sylvester also displays a wilful ignorance

Feigning interest in matters theological.

of the Eighth Commandment, passing up no opportunity to steal whatever food he can lay his paws on.

He is a curious cat – curious about other people. One of his great pleasures is greeting visitors; another is the disruption of groups meeting at the vicarage. He has two means of interrupting and disturbing gatherings. For the quiet, thoughtful occasions when a few are gathered for prayer, or are deep in theological consideration, Sylvester likes to hop nimbly up onto an unsuspecting lap. He settles down quietly, pretending to sleep. With a sleepy eye cocked at his chosen victim, he waits for a particularly quiet pause, and slowly stretches out, unsheathes his claws, and sinks them into knee or thigh with lightning speed. I believe the results are gratifying. I'm sure they don't extend to oaths, but they certainly inspire rapid movement and intake of breath amongst the recipients.

Banished from grace for this disruptive behaviour, Sylvester has another trick in his basket. He stalks around the house until he finds a window through which he can observe the proceedings, carefully manoeuvring himself so that he is unseen by Julian Scharf, but fully visible to visitors. Then follows a display of acrobatics and histrionics that would credit the finest melodrama. Nine times out of ten visitors will struggle to maintain their attention to the matters in hand and when (as they almost invariably do), they entirely lose the thread, Sylvester drops neatly out of sight before his owner can spot him.

*Sylvester in
the study.*

Buonaventura, Jacapone da Toda and Rufino

Shortly after his ordination as a Franciscan priest, Father Neil Hook was called on to officiate at his first wedding, in the Cathedral Parish Church of St John's, Brecon. Naturally apprehensive, he had double-checked that everything was as it should be. But he had reckoned without a cat. Buonaventura – known as Boni – plunged ten feet from a tree to engage in battle with the bride's train. The cat was delighted, the bride less so, but after the wedding photographer had disentangled Boni and the bride's dress, the wedding proceeded more or less to plan.

Boni had colonized the austere and imposing cathedral church of Brecon as a stray, flitting up and down the tower, lurking under pews and generally startling clergy and congregation alike, until the Heritage Centre staff stepped in, taking him into their care. Father Neil, then newly ordained, was presented with Boni as a moving-in present, and Boni had decided to make life as interesting as possible for him by hijacking his first ever wedding.

Being a Franciscan cat by adoption, Buonaventura takes full advantage of his patron saint's benign attitude towards animals. When not slumbering on his own woolly dog (originally called Albert but now known as 'flat Albert'), this burly and amiable cat has made the entire place his own, wandering about among visitors. He joins Father Neil when he takes a service in the local school (he is quietly ejected out of the window whilst the children have their eyes shut in

Boni on the Bishop's throne.

prayer), and frequently hops onto the Bishop's throne for an afternoon snooze.

Boni was most put out when two orphaned black and white cats came into his life, thanks to a veterinary nurse whose daughter was in the choir. These two kittens, with their white collars, had struck her as resembling little priests, and what better home could they

Rufi and Jax: angel spotting at the lychgate.

have than a Franciscan one? Named respectively Jacapone and Rufino, they watched in amazement as Boni indulged in astonishing but unsuccessful displays of bravado, including one spectacular failure to drag a raven in through the cat flap. (This raven has since conducted gang warfare against Boni, swooping down with its cohorts to deliver a fusillade of pecks whenever it spies the cat taking an outdoor rest.)

Realizing that he had not impressed the kittens one jot, Boni sulkily retired to further flatten flat Albert, whilst the two kittens, growing rapidly, and showing yet more spirited disrespect for the fraternal principles of their household, worked out that two against one can be pretty effective. Life settled down to an uneasy truce.

Jacapone (Jax) and Rufino (Rufi) soon developed that most frustrating of cat conditions, disdain of home cooking, and began to range wider to satisfy their over-sensitive palates. Rufi got to the Pilgrim's Restaurant first, drawn by the aromas of lunch preparation and the bonus of underfloor heating. He has a variety of strategies for getting into the restaurant, ranging from the subtle to outright frontal assault. And when entry is denied, Rufi sits on an antiquated coffin barrow staring mournfully at the diners through the windows, waiting for the door to open just a crack.

Jax has had to search wider to satisfy his foodie character traits. He has been rewarded amply by the discovery of banqueting facilities at the nearby castle, where his regular diet includes smoked salmon; he's a

Boni keeps his distance.

frequent visitor, and Father Neil makes regular trips to retrieve him.

Such high-grade surroundings are exploited to the full: all three cats can be found clambering over the lych-gate, slumbering on the sun-warmed stone of some ancient memorial, conducting vain pursuit of an insolent and more agile squirrel population – and of course, snoozing on the Bishop's throne.

It's not quite like having a dog at one's feet.

Jax waits for the restaurant door to open.

ST FAGAN'S, CARDIFF

Korky

Korky is a gentle soul whose great pleasure is to sit on the windowsill. She is often joined by a neighbourly mouse: they both sit in perfect peace, enjoying the warmth of the sun.

The name Korky conjured up for me a vision of a feisty, cheerful cat, a kindred spirit to the well-loved children's comic character, and I was somewhat disconcerted to see that at our introduction, Korky took one look at me, decided that I had come to murder her and retired in horror.

In vain I looked on the top floor of an apple box apartment lovingly created by Angela, journalist daughter of the Rev. Anthony and Mrs Anne Wintle. The search returned to the house, where a highly put-out Korky was coaxed from a temporary redoubt in Anthony Wintle's study.

Korky, like many church cats, chose her spot rather than being introduced to rectory life. She was discovered some four years ago, camped out in an old yew tree overlooking the church and rectory, and accepted with alacrity the offer of a warm, loving home. From the outset she reserved her most outspoken attentions to the task of feeding well, to the extent that she has persuaded the Wintle family to provide a chair for her at Sunday lunch. She has developed an uncanny ability to hear the word 'dinner', even when wandering through the churchyard of St Fagan's.

Korky is ... well ... cautious, and the reason for this is the presence of several ferocious feral cats, which have made her life a misery. So her passage to and from the rectory and church is a series of dashes from cover to cover, except when accompanying the Wintles, when she trails more like a dog than a cat.

Maybe this is a cat with literary aspirations – or at the least clerical inclinations. She often sorts through various papers and correspondence on the desk of

A horrified Korky makes her escape.

A wary Korky looks for intruders.

A rare public appearance in the churchyard.

Anthony Wintle. Her habit of eventually settling down to serious rest on stacks of marriage returns and letters from the Bishop does cause some administrative panics. Korky likes intelligent discourse, and is frequently seen in deep conversation with a doctor in the congregation.

I was told a touching story of how, one Christmas Eve, the Wintles and their congregation were leaving the church after the Christmas Eve service, and were startled to come across a minute, sickly and bedraggled kitten that had sought shelter in the church porch. I'm happy to be able to report that this foundling feline is now in the kindly care of a neighbouring family, making slow but steady progress to full health.

I wondered how Korky might take to having such a direct feline neighbour, given her current problems with the nearby feral cats. But Korky's preoccupations are almost entirely taken up with thinking about the time and content of her next meal.

ST MICHAEL AND ALL SAINTS', LEDBURY

Flossie and Corrie

I have a soft spot for these two chocolate-brown Burmese cats. They live opposite my studio, and at least one visits me frequently.

These two cats are consummate opportunists, who live with Alan and Judy Lloyd in the cobbled quaintness of Ledbury's Church Lane. They just about qualify as church cats: there are no clerics in the family, but, being of particularly intelligent disposition, the cats take great advantage of the fact that they live next to a magnificent church with a splendid churchyard. More importantly, they control access to it.

Corrie (Coriolanus) and Flossie (Florence) come from a family with a long tradition of Burmese cats, and share their home with an elderly spaniel called William, and Splodge, an arch-escapologist black and white cat. Splodge doesn't much care for Church Lane and its environs, and has decided that life in his old house, about four hundred yards away, is much more pleasant. He turns up there on a regular basis, expecting food, attention and somewhere comfortable to doze.

William the spaniel has his morning constitutional on a route that takes him through the churchyard and the overgrown grounds of the old grammar school. This routine caught the imagination of Flossie and Corrie, who decided that if a mere dog could take a regular walk, then so could they. And in the summer Alan Lloyd can be spotted, walking through the long grass, William at his heel, followed by two dew-soaked cat tails just visible above the grass. This canine/feline procession has become a regular feature of their life. Not surprisingly, the two cats decided that the church and its environs are their exclusive territorial

The west door remains closed to Flossie and Corrie.

Flossie flits through the churchyard.

possession: not only would they reserve it for themselves, but they would also actively oppose access by any other animals, in particular dogs.

Flossie and Corrie are shameless flirts, who spend much of their time simpering at tourists and charming the local Heritage Centre staff, and at the height of the tourist season, Church Lane echoes to the coo and gurgle of enchanted visitors. Flossie and Corrie have a number of standard tricks, such as rolling on their backs looking cute, feigning hunger, looking abandoned and my particular favourite, the Griffin pose, in which each cat flanks the church gates, nobly profiled and absolutely stock still. Dogs and their

owners should beware of this one. It precedes their other notable tableau, which I can only describe as the 'witch's cat on a broomstick' look, in which both cats are braced for speed and attack, claws extended and fur on end. This pose normally ends with a lightning concerted assault on some unsuspecting dog.

The dignity of St Michael's and Church Lane are frequently shattered by the terrified yelp of a dog as these two move in for the kill. The Lloyds are getting used to having irate dog owners protesting to them about keeping their cats under better control.

But drawing on their instinct for self-preservation, Flossie and Corrie have agreed, in the interests of continued and unrestricted access to the church and its grounds, to simply look the other way and feign abject terror every time the rector walks past with his dog.

These cats won't take no for an answer.

Dogs beware!

Flossie teeters on one of her favourite perches.

*Corrie never
gives up.*

HILFIELD FRIARY, NEAR DORCHESTER

Spats and Sponge

These two cats, although well loved by the community, have no intention of conforming to the gentle strictures of St Francis on the sanctity of life – especially when it comes to rabbits, mice and other unsuspecting mammals living within range of the Friary.

Hilfield Friary is one of those idyllic places that one comes across either by recommendation, or by taking a wrong turn down a lane that appears to lead to nowhere. Buried in the heart of the Dorset countryside, the Friary turns its back on the rush of modern life, offering religious retreats, and shelter for wayfaring men. Hardly the place for a pugilist cat called Dempsey, whose sole purpose in life was to empty the surrounding woodlands and fields of any trace of wildlife smaller than a sheep – and even they came under his baleful glare. As for dogs, they just steered clear.

But the brothers of the Order of St Francis are made of stern stuff, well used to awkward visitors, and Dempsey was partially assimilated into a more tranquil regime. Although his passing left the Friary in a quieter state, the community as a whole was still kindly disposed to cats, which was just as well, as local farm cats had their eyes on the Friary. In particular, one field cat adopted the Friary, giving birth to a healthy litter on a brother's bed. Of this litter, one kitten, Spats, stayed. I was introduced to Spats by Brother Aidan, who has had his fair share of living with cats – the bat-catching cats at the Friary's leprosarium in Africa, and two cats called Parker and Knoll (motto 'You want the chairs – we've gottem').

Spats colonized the whole Friary, working out a food routine that takes in Brother Aidan, Brother Philip and the community bursar, Fran, as well as various other brethren and visitors. This jolly black and white cat has his own comfort astonishingly well catered for. He can often be seen clambering up a wisteria to the top of an archway, from where he

Sponge had to pass the rope-girdle test.

negotiates an inclined tiled roof that gives access to the common room (usually providing the choice of three or four laps). A window gives access to Brother Philip's room (a comfortable chair, snacks and general cat love), and Spats hops nimbly through the ground-floor window leading to 95-year-old Brother Francis. Brother Aidan's room also offers a permanent food supply, bed, comfortable chair and, whenever possible, lap. For a while he had everything his own way, until it was decided to acquire a second cat.

Brother Robert set out with Fran the bursar, armed with a cat basket, to visit the local cat rescue centre. The idea was to apply a novel test of suitability for a Franciscan cat – the rope test. I thought this sounded rather alarming, but it was explained as a simple self-selection procedure. Brother Robert would swing his rope girdle in front of the cats that appealed to him. The cat that could work its way up to the top knot (implying obedience) would be the one for them. As it turned out, they didn't have an opportunity for choosing. One particularly enterprising white and black cat immediately launched itself in impressively maritime fashion up the rope girdle, thence up the rest of the habit, to settle on Brother Robert's shoulders, purring heavily. This insistent cat, working on the importance of a first impression, then swarmed down and installed itself, forepaws braced against possible eviction, in the Friary cat basket.

Spats did not accord the new arrival, Sponge, a truly Franciscan welcome and as a consequence, the two cats have divided the Friary into two exclusive territories. And Sponge has rather disgraced her initial eagerness to embrace the Franciscan ethic by continuing the programme of wildlife eradication started by Dempsey. The mice who scuttle about their business in the Friary's secret garden fervently wish that the brethren had kept it a better secret from Spats and Sponge.

The jovial Spats.

*Sponge takes an
un-Franciscan
interest in
wildlife.*

NORWICH CATHEDRAL

Jess and Boots

I make no apology for including Norwich Cathedral in *Church Cats*: it is a superb building and the Close teems with cats. Felix lives with two chickens and a dog, the Dean has cats, there's a lay clerk's cat called Squeaky and many others beside. But the cats I came to visit, Jess and Boots, live with Patrick and Katherine Williams-Dienes, in a Georgian terrace house overlooking the Cathedral Church.

This is a musical household: Patrick Williams is the librarian for the Hallé Orchestra, and Katherine Dienes is assistant organist at the Cathedral and director of the Cathedral Girls' Choir. With so much music around, it didn't surprise me that the cats have developed distinct musical preferences: Jess is particularly keen on Shostakovich. She's an intellectual sort of cat who makes a weekly trip to the Cathedral Music Office, where she sits by books of metaphysical poetry. She doesn't like her reading material moved, and my

Jess: a cat with musical taste.

attempt to shift a book met with a quick but sharp nip of disapproval. Jess arranges herself within earshot of the keyboard on which Katherine scores vocal arrangements for the choir, twitching her ears in approval or criticism, Katherine is not sure which. Jess also sits in on the Girls' Choir.

Boots, on the other hand, is much more emotional and sensitive, having a distinct inclination towards Mahler. I must say that this rather surprised me, as Mahler demands a degree of robustness on the part of the listener: Boots' reaction to having a photographer in the house was anything but robust. She gaped in horror as I opened a camera bag, and the sight of a camera had her hurtling in terror up the stairs. She eventually sought refuge behind one of next door's chickens. I wasn't fooled; Boots doesn't realize that chickens don't have long, furry black tails.

The cats are sublimely content in their cathedral home, despite the occasional visits from well-meaning neighbourly cats (and one or two close calls with some not so well-disposed cats too).

The cat flap should have been the key to full participation in Close life, but it remained a total mystery for eighteen months, despite patient attempts by Katherine and Patrick to explain its use. Jess and Boots would stare in amazement at Patrick and Katherine demonstrating how one pushes the flap with one's head.

Listening to a new choral arrangement.

Shortly after taking up residence, Jess and Boots were visited by Fred, a jolly ginger cat belonging to a nearby retired headmistress, who had no such reservations about using cat flaps. They didn't hear him come in; he inadvertently walked straight past them and began to sun himself on the balcony. Jess and Boots awoke to the sight of this ginger gent at the window, and nearly trampled each other to death in their efforts to get out of the room.

Life has been full of little surprises for the cats. Shortly after they decided to make use of the cat flap, Katherine held a barbecue in her garden for the Girls' Choir, where pride of place was given to the new choir mascot, a four-foot-high bear perched on the garden wall. (Jess and Boots had long dismissed the previous mascot, Denzel the Duck, as an irrelevancy.) The cats were debating how to make off with a frankfurter when they suddenly spied this enormous bear frowning down: both cats jumped so high that they almost cleared the roof of the potting shed. Now they keep a wary eye on the bear whenever it is spotted in the house. Not that it deters them from their everyday routines, which comprise walking up and down the keyboard, cutting off telephone calls, sending blank faxes to random numbers, and finishing up the breakfast cereals.

Boots couldn't believe she'd been found.

ST MARY'S, LITTLE BIRCH

Toscanini and Pudding

There are many churches in Britain's rural depths, but few so peaceful and secluded as that at Little Birch, in Herefordshire. As with so many country churches, this one is part of a group, and no longer has a resident parson. But it is still used by the local community, and has been adopted by two local cats as their adventure playground.

Some years back, Judith Coles moved into a house overlooking the church. Judith was no stranger to cats, having left several in the care of her mother whilst she settled in to her new home. Life without cats was not good, and she was joined by two young felines, Pudding and Toscanini (Nini for short).

For a while, these two cats charged around the house, mostly between the hours of midnight and 3 a.m., a habit that even the most ardent cat lover can lose patience with.

Pudding greets parishioners at the gate.

Judith had occasion to speak severely with this lively pair. 'Why,' she asked, 'don't you go out a bit more often?' This subtle plea for nocturnal peace was completely ignored, until the unannounced arrival of two strays, who were not so young, rather less patient than Judith, and very large.

The first, Bruiser, is a dreadnought of a cat he feline equivalent of a heavyweight boxer, as is the second, Tabby. The two latter arrivals wanted nothing more than a comfortable hearth, food, and peace. It was the 'peace' bit that finally persuaded Pudding and Nini that there might be some point to spending time out of the house. Reluctant exploration turned to enthusiasm as the two cats discovered the delights of the neighbouring churchyard, in which they began to spend more and more time. Stone gravestones, boundary walls and the ubiquitous yew tree provided an ideal playground, as well as great cover for hunting. The two cats embraced the church as their own.

It was Pudding who discovered that there was more to church life than vaulting over tombstones and streaking up the yew tree – there were times when a lot of people came too. Pudding took on the role of escort, assisting with car parking, greeting folk at the gate, accompanying them into the church, and generally seeing to their (and his) comfort. He sometimes pushes his luck a bit far, but six forced exits from one wedding haven't deterred him one bit. Sunday services are slightly easier, but he has discovered that it doesn't always pay to advertise his presence too heavily: better to curl up quietly under a pew near one of the heaters.

Given all this involvement in church life, it is rather embarrassing to report that Pudding in particular has displayed a strong irreligious streak to his nature, steadfastly refusing to attend a Service for the Blessing of Animals. This may have had something to do with the presence of an equally irreligious German Shepherd dog. Further evidence of this cat's secular nature can be observed in his terror-stricken flight at the slightest sound from the church bells. I am told that Pudding, in common with most church cats, considers that whereas cats are entirely entitled to attend Pet Services, dogs would benefit more from attending exorcisms.

Toscanini puts in a rare appearance.

Not everyone opens up for Pudding.

TEWKESBURY ABBEY

Rosa Mystica (retired)

Until I met Rosa Mystica, the only cat I had come across that had been ejected from its home territory was the Westminster Abbey cat Biggles, whose habit of savaging tourists eventually brought about compulsory retirement from the Abbey precincts.

Rosa was once also required to leave Tewkesbury Abbey in somewhat undignified circumstances, being summarily ejected by an indignant churchwarden, and landing by accident in the Bishop of Gloucester's arms.

Rosa Mystica was a stray, who had haunted the flood-prone fields adjacent to Tewkesbury Abbey before discovering the sanctuary of the groundsman's shed in the Abbey grounds. An archaeological dig became her main daily occupation: she would spend hours watching sympathetically as members of the dig carefully brushed away dirt from areas of particular interest, and enthusiastically supplemented the endeavours of the team at night with her own brand of feline excavations. For six months she slept in the groundsman's shed, being cared for by the sacristan.

Life at the Abbey was good. It provided her with unlimited opportunities for comfort. The services and concerts at Tewkesbury Abbey provided a sea of laps from which to choose, and Rosa would slink underneath the congregation or audience looking for a capacious lap, preferably one with a folded coat on it. Having selected her lap, she'd nimbly hop up, settle down and sleep, occasionally twitching a critical ear

Bea viewed Rosa's retirement with mixed feelings.

35

Ever watchful,
Rosa keeps her
eye on Bea.

during the sermon, or being woken with a start at the beginning of a passage of fortissimo.

She became so familiar with the Abbey routines that it was not unusual to see Rosa make a nonchalant appearance on the altar, or to find her wandering round the Abbey with a group of visitors. Rosa was oblivious to her good fortune in getting such unlimited access to the Abbey church: a predecessor, Smudge, a black and white cat belonging to a retired clergyman, had howled long, hard and very unsuccessfully outside the Abbey doors, trying to get into Sunday services.

However, Rosa's days as the church cat were numbered; she had by this time been housed by Joanna Chorley, who lived across a busy main road from the Abbey. Concern for her safety was expressed, and the final decision to retire her from Abbey life was taken shortly before one bonfire night (the adjacent

With Bea inside, Rosa relaxes.

water meadows are the scene of a massive bonfire and firework display).

No matter, for having already achieved some degree of fame, being featured in the *Church Times* as well as the parish magazine, Rosa was to enjoy a quieter life of luxury, and eventually moved to live with Joanna Chorley's daughter, Susan, where she now enjoys a luxurious, if not entirely peaceful, retirement.

She no longer has to contend with the hazards of traffic, fireworks or cantankerous churchwardens, but she does have feline competition, in the form of Bea and Simpkin. Simpkin is a forest cat, adept at opening any door and window, whose sole aim in life is to be uninterrupted. Bea, however, is a different proposition, an 'artful dodger' of a cat who can lift saucepan lids quietly, and is now working out how to open oven doors without getting burnt. This entertaining, if slightly villainous, cat lost no opportunity to let Rosa Mystica know who was boss, and seized every chance to deliver a resounding cuff round Rosa's ears. Rosa Mystica handled all this with aplomb, hunting vigorously, eating quickly, and settling to warm in the unassailable fastness of a kitchen grill.

Tewkesbury Abbey now has a new visitor, in the shape of a small, black and white pub cat who, having gazed at the Abbey through an upstairs window for many months, has decided to investigate the more sensitive side of her nature. Tewkesbury Abbey is in the process of acquiring yet another church cat.

Bea ponders her next move.

*Rosa on
guard again.*

ST LAURENCE'S, LUDLOW

Amber, Mittens and Moppet

About four and a half years ago the Curnew family moved from Bristol to the parish of St Laurence, Ludlow, bringing with them two cats, Mittens and Moppet. Moving had been traumatic enough, and Moppet had decided to add to the general levels of stress by disappearing, only reappearing at the last minute. She was seized by daughter Miranda and placed firmly in the car.

Their new home was the old rectory, lying in the shadow of the imposing parish church of St Laurence, whose origins date back to the twelfth century. Shortly after moving in, Mittens and Moppet also found that they had moved into a thriving cat community, meeting for the first time, and not entirely without incident, Mr Ross, Sammy, Thomas and Jumbly, all of whom had prior claims to being the cats of St Laurence. Mittens went missing. The Curnews' eldest daughter Rose, who had fought a long battle to persuade the family that a tabby cat was exactly what the family needed, searched high and low. Posters were distributed about the town, but there was no sign of Mittens. Fortunately his howls were eventually heard: he was trapped in a deep pit, and Rose rushed to the rescue with a ladder.

One would have thought that with all this feline activity, other cats would steer clear, but lurking in the undergrowth was a ginger and white cat. At the optimum moment, this cat crept out from under a bush, slunk over the lawn and slid through the Curnews' back-door cat flap. Being kind folk, the family decided

Moppet, caught on the stairs.

to let this new arrival stay, and so Amber joined Moppet and Mittens.

This was not the easiest of adoptions. Amber rewarded the Curnews' kindness by spraying through the house, which behaviour was swiftly rewarded by a visit to the vet for irreversible alterations. Back at the

*Amber's dainty
table manners
don't fool the
other cats.*

rectory, with Amber in the charge of youngest daughter Imogen, all was not well between the three cats. Amber rather smugly demonstrated a surprising sophistication of table manners, charming everyone – except Mittens and Moppet – with his ability to drink milk from his own mug. In fact milk was a near obsession, along with yoghurt, butter and cheese: if it had any trace of milk, Amber would eat or drink it. Mittens and Moppet were not impressed. They gazed on with disdain while Amber paraded his *savoir-faire* in the food department. An uneasy truce settled, with all cats claiming certain areas of the (fortunately large) rectory as safe havens; but even now caution is the watchword, all three cats exchanging deeply felt hisses as they pass on the stairs.

This is a situation that many cat families will recognize, and leads to all sorts of complicated eating arrangements in the kitchen. One cat goes out while the other eats, then comes back and another cat goes out, and so on – no fraternal feline sentiments here.

In a diplomatic attempt to defuse the situation, Imogen persuaded Amber to attend a Pet Service with her and, while various dogs howled along with the hymns, Amber lay demurely in his basket, paws together as he received his blessing. Regrettably the blessing seemed to have little effect, for on re-entering the rectory, Amber delivered a resounding cuff to both other cats, stalked into the kitchen, ate all their food, and installed himself unassailably on the central heating boiler.

The blessing had little effect on Amber.

ST WULFRAM'S, GRANTHAM

Tara, a.k.a. Cheeky

When the Rev. Christopher Andrews and his wife Christine arrived at the Georgian rectory of St Wulfram's, the last thing on their minds was the question of a pet. They had never had a cat, nor did they particularly want one. The family was, if anything, more inclined towards dogs, and the only pet so far had been a guinea pig belonging to the children, Samuel and Harriet.

Unbeknown to the Andrews, fate had

Cheeky had already adopted the rectory garden.

decreed differently. Living wild in the rambling rectory garden, there was a black and white cat that had deliberately hidden when her previous owners had moved out of the area. The verger had already come across Tara, strolling up the nave, attracted perhaps by the bustle of children from the nearby school or the statue on the West Front of Bishop Hine, showing a cat reaching up to play with his rope girdle.

The Andrews soon noticed this cat, lurking in the shrubs and flitting silently around the garden. They assumed that this was a 'visitor' from a nearby house. Tara was a sort of visitor: the cheeky kind that never knows when it has outstayed its welcome. Summer drew to a close and early autumn brought a chill to the air. Tara knew that it was time for her to find somewhere warm in which to pass the winter. She completed her reconnaissance of the rectory, and as the weather turned, made her first move.

The Andrews had not taken much notice of the cat flap in the kitchen door, and when they came in after a shopping trip, were puzzled to hear strange noises coming from upstairs. Reassuring themselves that there was no evidence of a spectral presence, they searched for the source, coming across Cheeky sitting nonchalantly at the head of the stairs. The cat was pleasantly but firmly escorted out of the house. Feeling fairly certain that she must have another home nearby, they locked the cat flap and enquired locally as to whether anyone was missing a cat. It was at this

Cheeky won by sheer determination.

point that they found out that the cat was called Tara, and had refused to move with her original family. In the meantime Tara, a.k.a. Cheeky, had worked out how to unlock the cat flap, and came in again. Yet again she was escorted out. She came back. This war of attrition on the cat's part continued: the Andrews capitulated, and Cheeky found a new home.

Living with their first cat was eventful. Cheeky made no concessions, launching merciless attacks on visiting dogs, getting into endless fights outdoors, and dragging in some fairly unspeakable offerings. She even inspired admonishing letters from other members of the family about the perils of owning an unpredictable cat. Oblivious to the controversy surrounding her new-found residence, Cheeky indulged in the joys of table-top soccer and marbles, and ruthlessly disposed of the resident cellar mice. Her penchant for the outdoors is still strong, and she enjoys nothing more than joining in a game of rounders or tennis.

The Andrews seem slightly bemused as to how they came to be a cat family. But on balance, Cheeky seems to have brought pleasure rather than pain – although I'm not sure that this would be the verdict of the local squirrels and birds, or the mice that used to inhabit the cellars.

The other garden residents make themselves scarce!

Bishop Hines' stone cat.

47

A feline benediction.

Cheeky is oblivious to controversy.

ST MARY-LE-BOW, LONDON

Minou

As far as the Rev. Victor Stock can tell, Minou is the only church cat in London's Square Mile. She was not always alone, having two sisters, Ash and Wednesday, but they preferred the quieter corners of North London's Highbury district.

This fortunate mackerel-marked tabby cat lives at an exceptionally well-connected church (its sister church is Trinity, parish church of Manhattan's Wall Street), and St Mary-le-Bow, built on the site of a Norman church, is surrounded by legend and famed for its bells. The original medieval bells sounded the end of the nightly curfew, and are said to be those that persuaded Dick Whittington to return to the city to become three times Lord Mayor, accompanied, of course, by his faithful and artful cat. Thus Minou has the interesting position of being the apostolic successor to Dick Whittington's cat, and being born almost right over the Bow Bells, could be said to have more than a touch of 'true cockney'.

Whereas Dick Whittington's cat wandered at will, Minou haunts the church and rector's lodgings, flitting through a Disneyesque city roofscape. Traffic in London has changed somewhat since Dick Whittington's day, and on a scale of one to ten, Victor Stock has rated her chance of surviving the surrounding swirl of nearby traffic at minus one. She is certainly the only cat I have come across so far who has an enchanting rooftop garden more or less to herself, and London's wily pigeons get a big surprise when they glide down from the church tower to sunbathe in Minou's roof garden.

With this extensive enclosed territory, and plenty of company when she chooses, Minou lives a stress-free life. She'll happily sit in on meetings and interviews with parishioners and visitors, and is not above offering some criticism of the proceedings when moved to do so. Although her experience of the outside world is a bird's-eye view of Cheapside, she is by no means

Minou's conversation has little spiritual significance.

*Life at
the top.*

subject to close confinement, and frequently strolls downstairs into the wood-panelled parish offices, where she holds, so I'm told, lengthy conversations with the office staff. If such conversations take place, I don't think that they have much spiritual significance, for although she frequently follows Victor Stock to the church for quiet morning and evening prayers, she displays not the slightest sense of reverence. She jumps over the pews, inspects the memorial monuments in a rather desultory manner, and generally seems rather impatient to get back to her rooftop redoubt. She is, Victor Stock says, 'a most irreverent and irreligious creature'.

A most inquisitive cat.

Enjoying the winter sunshine.

HOLY TRINITY, STRATFORD-UPON-AVON

Sammie and Rosie

Holy Trinity Church, beside the River Avon, is the final resting place of William Shakespeare, who was a lay rector of the church. It is a place of dignity and beauty, full of history, none of which has rubbed off at all on the Holy Trinity cats, Sammie and Rosie.

Sammie and Rosie live with the Rev. Peter and Mrs Ruth Holliday and their daughters Juliette and Molly. The Hollidays have had cats before, well-travelled ones too, that regularly clambered into the family car: they especially enjoyed Christmases at the Hollidays' house in the Malvern countryside.

After the cats died, Peter Holliday decided that the family had enough animals to look after – two dogs and an assortment of rabbits. This was in response to that well-known syndrome of children who would die to have an animal, and immediately after their dearest wish is answered, seem to suffer amnesia, especially on the subject of feeding and cleaning out of litter.

Juliette was convinced that having more cats was in the family's best interest, and spent several months persecuting her father by making meowing sounds whenever they passed a cat. Gradually she wore down his resolve and one day, when news came of a litter of kittens at a neighbouring vicarage, Peter Holliday gracefully gave way: two small kittens were soon installed at the rectory.

An initial stand off between the dogs and kittens gradually gave way to grudging acceptance – the kittens being the aggressors rather than the dogs.

Sammie and Rosie were delighted to discover the rabbits in the garden. They saw them as great big furry toys. Until, that is, the great big furry toys got out of their run, and started chasing the kittens round the garden. The dogs liked this game and joined in with gusto. This *mélange* usually performed in front of Peter Holliday's study window, and was the cause of many typing errors and lost trains of thought.

As the kittens grew, so the garden rumpus calmed down. Sammie grew ever bolder with the dogs, giving Gemma the Labrador a hearty bash every time they passed. Rosie, being the smaller of the two, was more

Rosie: one of the garden mélange.

*Sammy waits
for Rosie to
walk into the
ambush.*

A perfect maze for a cat.

cautious, and still is. She's still trying to encourage her growth rate by sleeping in the greenhouse.

Sammie has been drawing inspiration from other sources, and the spectacle of boats on the river has encouraged him to conduct his own experiments with water. The river is a little extreme, but the wash basins are something else altogether. Sammie curls up in them, and invariably plunges into the basin over which family members are cleaning their teeth. Consequentially there is much unexpected swallowing of hot mint toothpaste, and some rather unclerical exclamations. Both Rosie and Sammie are expert at ambushing each other, and spend hours prowling along the long lines of garden hedges, leaping out when least expected.

Sammie seems to have imbibed Stratford's dramatic atmosphere and has developed a love of melodrama, particularly in the form of surprise appearances. One such took place during an ecumenical gathering one Christmas in the Hollidays' sitting room. Both Rosie and Sammie had offered endless help with trimming the Christmas tree, knocking off glass balls, yanking at garlands and tinsel, and helping to turn off the lights by chewing through the cable. Not satisfied with this, Sammie decided one afternoon to explore the deeper recesses of the Christmas tree. Having settled down for a rather prickly nap, he woke at dusk to find the room had filled with people from the various churches in the area. The tree was lit up, the lights were dimmed. Sammie stretched and the tree shivered slightly. Visitors became aware that the tree was swaying. Sammie decided to say 'hello', and made his unsteady way along a branch, the tree pitching increasingly, decorations by this time rattling and crashing to the ground. Sammie leaped for safety, shooting out of the Christmas tree like a tinsel-draped comet. Those of a sensitive disposition were forgiven for wondering about the Christmas ghost. For Peter Holliday, however, it was just one more disruption in an otherwise ordered life.

MALMESBURY ABBEY

Tano

The Malmesbury Abbey cat is one the most patrician-looking of the church cats I have come across. But despite his aristocratic appearance, this gigantic chocolate tabby point Siamese is a most amiable fellow, one in a line of Siamese that have lived with David and Christine Littlefair. Tano is the Littlefairs' fifth cat and his name is Swahili for 'five'. Tano came to Malmesbury with another Siamese, Tanu, who had come as a rescue cat. She'd been severely mistreated, and only became manageable after Christine Littlefair, in desperation, had laid her hands on her and prayed. The transformation was not far short of miraculous, and from being mortal enemies, Tano and Tanu became the closest of companions.

Their new home was a vicarage built by the old town walls, close to the Abbey. Tano in particular took the opportunity to do what he likes most – hunt. With a wilderness running down to the river and the cloister gardens close by, he was in seventh heaven. He was particularly proud of some of his trophies, and liked to bring them into the house. Most cats strew the fruits of their hunting all over the place. Not Tano: he has a curious predilection for order, preferring to store his trophies – a squirrel under the dining room carpet, a whole legion of mice carefully tucked under his bed. His one known lapse from this penchant for order was a turkey carcass. He'd nipped quietly into the kitchen after Christmas lunch, retiring discreetly upstairs with the remains of the turkey. He must have panicked when the carcass was found to be missing – it was hastily jammed under the bed.

It would be misleading to give the impression that all Tano does is hunt. He talks incessantly, as do all Siamese, and dies for a good tickle. (For most cats this is a gentle affair, but with the gigantic Tano it's more like an amiable wrestling bout.) He also takes an interest in the model

Tano, the amiable aristocat.

railway encircling part of the garden. He paces the track by moonlight, and his ability to leap out of the way of an express train would have earned him a stunt job in the film industry. Occasionally the train comes off worst, with the 2.00 p.m. Special from Malmesbury Vicarage being swatted off the rails or being held, wheels skidding wildly, by an unyielding forepaw.

Tanu died, leaving Tano in despair: he still calls mournfully, for he's never known life without a cat to cuddle. Rain seems to bring on the blues; he sits on the kitchen window and looks out, heaving deep sighs. But he has loving humans for company, and makes absolutely sure that everyone in the house

He prefers the garden prayer groups.

Tano holds up the 2.00 p.m. Special.

knows he is around. Tano makes a unique contribution to prayer groups, punctuating silence with a chorus of meows. This gets a bit much sometimes, and Tano is ushered out to the kitchen, where his sounds redouble, but in more muffled manner. Tanu liked prayer groups too, preferably ones in the garden, where she would startle the assembled company by appearing from nowhere, hop up onto a spare seat, and sit stock still with her eyes shut tight.

David Littlefair is less than convinced by his cats' apparent devoutness. In support of his reservations he cites the appalling language used by Tano, in animated discussion with neighbouring cats over the subject of territorial rights.

A rare moment of quiet for the garrulous Tano.

ST PETER & ST PAUL'S, NORTH CURRY, SOMERSET

Little Arthur

Little Arthur is a stocky mackerel-marked tabby, who lives in a Georgian rectory with the Rev. Charles Townsend and his wife, Gillian. I'm curious as to how names are chosen for cats: this is the first cat that I know of who has been named after an island (one of the Scilly Isles, off the Cornish coast)! Little Arthur is the surviving one of two. His brother Quinquagesima had the curious habit of disappearing into the innermost recesses of the organ loft when annoyed or upset. Only full diapasons on the great organ could budge him.

They came as kittens in the fond hope that the Townsends' older cat, MumPuss, would take to mothering them. It didn't work, for she retired to sulk in the upper regions of the house, emerging only to box the kittens' ears. MumPuss eventually went to the tranquillity of a relative's house, leaving the two kittens to battle for pole position.

There was a lot of sibling rivalry between these two. Little Arthur had to have first go at the food, while Quinqua would wait outside. Arthur would then sally forth into the garden, to be boxed around the ears by his brother, who in his turn then went into the kitchen and fed. And if by rare chance the two cats did feed at the same time, they would spend as much time carefully eyeing the size of each other's portions as they did with the actual eating. With hunting it was the same. Both cats would lock onto opposite ends of their 'find', and Little Arthur, being the lighter of the two, would often find himself left holding what Charles Townsend discreetly refers to as 'an empty pair of bunny trousers'. Arthur was and still is particularly good at finding warm spots to sleep in. Quinquagesima would follow Arthur, let him find a good spot for a nap, and then climb in on top, gradually squeezing Little Arthur

Little Arthur picks all the best spots for a nap.

out. Another equally acceptable resting-place would then be found, and the same process would happen all over again. The two cats ended up quite exhausted; there was never any time for a proper rest.

Both cats were intrigued by the sounds of exotic birds from a neighbour's house, and the Townsends wondered if it would be long before an irate visitor arrived to complain of the cats despatching various rare birds. The tropical cacophony that the birds set up was their security: it terrified Quinquagesima to the extent that he'd seek refuge on Gillian Townsend's shoulders.

Little Arthur has become more contrary in his latter years, plaintively meowing at the sight of the milk jug, then stalking off to drink water if offered the milk in a dish. With Quinqua's passing, at least Little Arthur can snooze undisturbed, although he is a little lonely now that his brotherly adversary is no longer around. He passes time on the kitchen windowsill trying to catch a glimpse of neighbouring felines. (If this is done out of yearning for feline company, then it is yet further evidence of a contrary nature, for he curses roundly when another cat comes into view.)

There's no doubt that Little Arthur enjoys life around the church and rectory. He's a keen bird watcher, and his eyes almost start out of his head when a heron alights in the garden. But he does miss his brother. It was much more fun to lurk underneath the dining table hoping for a wayward scrap when he knew that there would be a scuffle for it.

On the way to church.

64

Little Arthur still misses his brother.

ST WILFRED'S, SELBY

Amy

The fact that Amy is nearly toothless does not deter a nightly parade of admirers, who sit expectantly on the churchyard wall, calling in vain for her attentions.

Amy came to live with David and Christine Reynolds through the RSPCA and a local vet. She had already been rejected by two homes: she had been in such poor health when first found that most of her teeth had to be removed. The vet had almost given up finding a home for her, when a request for a cat came from the Reynolds. Amy didn't give them a choice when they came to view her – she leapt onto Christine Reynolds' shoulder, and hung on for dear life.

Amy was lucky to come across the Reynolds. They had already rescued one feral cat – Smokey – who had been thrown out one bonfire night, and was found under a van. Amy's toothlessness didn't deter them one bit. There were some delicate introductions to be made when they arrived home, but son David undertook to introduce the cat to Sammie, a friendly retriever, Dolly (a terrier who had been born under a gooseberry bush, really!), and Jesse, a collie pup. Amy was not deterred, and in short order biffed each one of the dogs to show that there would be no messing with her. Having sorted out the dogs, Amy had to deal with her other great problem – agoraphobia. She was simply terrified of open spaces, and constantly searched for tiny boxes and cupboards into which she could wedge herself. Patience on the part of the Reynolds gradually helped overcome her fears, and before very long she was strolling at David Reynolds' heels through the rectory garden and into the churchyard, in company with Jesse the collie.

Not content with cats and dogs, the Reynolds also acquired a Cornish donkey called Ned, whose speciality is braying loud and persistent greetings to the parishioners. He's a wonderful prop for the children's Christmas services. Amy likes Ned, especially when he is in his stable: she makes a nest of straw just out of reach of his back hooves. Ned, on the other hand, is not quite so sure about Amy: she gets lots of curious looks from the donkey, particularly when she's trying to climb onto his back. Ned may be a source of

Amy: a toothless cat with plenty of bite.

warmth, but he might one day become a surprise launchpad.

Amy gets so excited about life these days that there are times when she seems to forget altogether that she's a cat. Particularly confusing is her recent habit of planting herself in flowerpots. This is fine in the winter, but her popularity wanes considerably in the summer when she plants herself in the midst of a precious horticultural specimen.

Amy takes root.

Amy enjoys being chased around the churchyard.

Of all the animals, it is with Jesse that Amy has formed the closest friendship, and one of their favourite games is when Jesse chases Amy round the garden and churchyard. Amy concludes this game by swarming up the nearest tree. Unfortunately, in the heat of the moment she doesn't always check that she can get down again. But Jesse saves the day by rushing back to tell the family that Amy is stuck – again.

Amy successfully overcame her agoraphobia.

ST PETER AND ST PAUL'S, PICKERING

Pushkin

Pushkin's great age – nineteen – and her considerable agility accord her the position of Senior Cat in *Church Cats*. Nineteen is a considerable age for a cat. She still prowls the rectory garden, albeit a little stiffly, but in the autumn of her life she has eschewed her love of hunting. Nowadays the blackbirds hop up to her in greeting rather than fleeing in alarm.

Pushkin came to the Hewitt family at Lastingham. Brenda Hewitt told me of her pedigree – 'pure-bred farm cat'. It was a pedigree that had a very special use. The Hewitts had just moved, in the midst of a particularly cold and snowy January, into the rectory at Lastingham. On the first night the family realized, from the frantic scurrying of little feet in the attic, that a legion of mice had moved in too. The Hewitts' daughter Claire knew of a litter of kittens on the nearby farm, and the following day she struggled through the snow to view the litter: she picked the smallest, and Pushkin came to stay.

Priorities were important to this fierce little kitten, and the first of those was to sort out the family dogs, which she did in record time, reducing Barnabas the deerhound to a whimpering wreck. Pushkin has never had any trouble with dogs: a quick swipe around the nose, some ferocious spitting, and they become totally compliant. The Hewitts' second deerhound, Barnabas II, was reduced to being a bed for Pushkin: every night she would clamber onto his back and settle down purring contentedly. Even when she sank her

Pushkin: pure-bred farm cat.

Food has been a life-long interest for Pushkin.

claws into his back, he just gritted his teeth and held the position. Pushkin is a survivor: she has endured a twenty-four hour crawl home after being hit by a motorcycle, and has actually appeared with a fox snare set fast around her.

Pushkin lived up to her farm pedigree, and hunted relentlessly: birds, rats, bats and rabbits were all fair game to her, and every night she'd struggle up the drainpipe, dragging her prey into the kitchen. Things got so bad that members of the family fought to be last into the kitchen each morning.

At Francis Hewitt's last parish, Pushkin and Barnabas II would patrol with him to and from the church in solemn procession, with Pushkin checking out the tourists, and developing an avid interest in any burial preparations. She was fascinated by the sexton's activities: a man who dug holes six feet deep deserved serious respect. This interest became so acute that she would sit and watch burials whenever they took place. On one occasion it all became too much for Pushkin. She rocketed through the legs of assorted mourners and undertakers who were in the process of interring a loved one's ashes, and leapt into the hole. Luckily the widow was a cat lover, as had been the deceased.

Food has been a life-long interest. Pushkin eats the dog's food, appears as if by magic for family lunches and dinners, and views the cooker as a sort of comestible jukebox: push a button and food appears. She has occasionally overstepped the mark: on one

occasion a chocolate roulade was left out overnight, and the following morning even Pushkin had a hard time explaining how her footprints had appeared in a straight line from one end of the dish to the other.

Always hoping the sexton will dig a new hole.

Nowadays the birds simply hop up to Pushkin.

The most senior of church cats.

BUCKFAST ABBEY

Blackie, Mummy Cat and Tiger

The peaceful setting of the Benedictine community of Buckfast Abbey is a perfect place for a cat, with gardens, a river, mill-race and woodlands, and the kindly attentions of the community. Some twelve years ago the Guestmaster, Brother Joseph, noticed a grey and white cat that had made its home in the cellars under the monastery kitchens. In due course this cat had a litter of kittens, one of which she proudly brought up into the monastery courtyard for Brother Joseph to admire. She presented a black kitten that perfectly complemented the Benedictine habit. The rest of the kittens were given away, but Blackie stayed, and has lived for four years with her mother in the warmth and shelter of the cellars.

Mummy Cat still retains a feral wariness.

Like many mother-and-daughter relationships, theirs has its ups and downs: every now and then there is a definite tension between them, best observed as they jostle each other for the snuggest spot amongst the shrubs. Mummy Cat still retains a feral wariness of humans, and does not allow people to touch her. But she will happily join one for a walk. She often accompanies Father Paulinus when he walks along the riverside, and sprints over to Brother Joseph at meal times (which are as regular as everything else in the daily monastic routine: the cats get into a complete muddle when the clocks are changed). Blackie, on the other hand, whom Brother Joseph handled from an early age (she found his hood to be a great place in which to snooze), enjoys a good cuddle and stalks, tail held high, up to anyone. Both cats keep pretty much to the immediate precincts of the Abbey, eschewing public areas (although they often trot along at Brother Joseph's heels as he walks to the iron gates that separate the public and private areas of the monastery).

Mummy Cat and Blackie have not had things entirely their way. They were joined for a while by an extremely large and friendly duck who preempted any unnecessary feline aggression by administering a series of sharp pecks. After the cats had got over their astonishment at this audacious bird, the creatures would eat together outside the kitchen window.

Cat relationships here are not always conducted in the best monastic tradition. Mummy Cat and her daughter Blackie have been joined by another cat, a debonair tabby called Tiger. Tiger never really got into the spirit of fellowship, and the gardens echo to some pretty unholy rows as Tiger chases Blackie furiously up a tree, with Mummy Cat in hot maternal pursuit, fiercely defending her offspring. Tiger has her own mentor, Father Richard, the Prior, who feeds her daily away from the kitchen windowsill favoured by the other two. Tiger also has her own wandering territory, around the perimeter of the workshops that produce Buckfast's famous Tonic Wine. All three cats have been known to chase the famous Buckfast bees, and have good reason to be grateful that Brother Adam has bred his bees to be gentle!

Neither Mummy Cat nor Tiger has made any serious attempt to get into the enclosure. But Blackie is more adventurous: she sits by the doorway like a medieval doorkeeper, and if there's a chance, she's in like a shot. She has been shut in the cloisters several times, where her black coat combines with the dim light to turn her into a perfect stumbling block for anyone lost in contemplative thought. And if such a person should, after picking himself up, continue to ignore her, she adds her voice to that of the plainchant – at which point she is unmonastically ejected. All three cats have been known to stand outside yowling in unison, so something of the monastic life has rubbed off. The other concession that the cats make to monastic life is that they don't hunt birds, who in their turn take no notice whatsoever of the cats.

Blackie enjoys the cloistered life.

Tiger never developed a sense of community.

*The feline
doorkeepers of
Buckfast Abbey.*

ST MICHAEL'S CHURCH, ALNWICK

Sandy, Antigone and Pooh

S andy, the Burmese cat belonging to Canon
Murray and Mrs Deborah Haig, loses the age
record in *Church Cats* by six months. But at eighteen years six months he still braves the chilly
breezes that sweep off the North Sea through St
Michael's Church.

Sandy had a controversial introduction to church
life. He was noisily conceived during a Sunday service,
just outside the church doors. It was a hot summer's
day, and all the church doors were open: in the midst
of the first hymn, a chorus of yowls and howls broke
out. The choir and organist faltered, then picked up
again with renewed vigour and greater volume, but
nothing could mask the appalling sounds coming
from outside. After a while the noise abated, the service continued, and into the church strolled Sandy's
mother-to-be, TinTin. One of the altar servers discreetly swept her up, and deposited her outside. After
a few minutes TinTin crept in again, this time
through the open vestry door. With great aplomb the
same altar server picked her up and somewhat less cer-
emoniously dumped her outside, swiftly closing the
vestry door, whilst a member of the congregation
hastily shut the main doors. The congregation
sweltered through the remainder of the service.

Defying the best efforts of a charismatic curate's
prayers, Sandy's birth was fraught, and after a long
struggle he emerged into the world, looking the pic-
ture of gentility. Sandy's innocence was shattered by
his encounters with the Haigs' other cat, Sid Vicious,

Tigger holds court in the rectory garden.

whom he met on the stairs. The two engaged in a
furious battle for staircase supremacy: Sid won, and
Sandy thereafter found his way up to the first floor via
a drainpipe. While all this was going on, TinTin was
quietly engaged in protracted correspondence with
Bishop Mervyn Stockwood's cat Midge. Both cats
complained to each other about life in general, and in
particular how rude some people were about their
names and provenance. But TinTin's career as a regular correspondent was to be abruptly cut short.

All sorts of disasters struck. Sid was run over,
TinTin was stolen and the Haigs decided to bring in
some company for Sandy, in the form of two Siamese

cats. Antigone (Tigger for short) and Pooh were both poorly kittens. One had cat flu, the other had a hole in her heart: both required constant nursing, and Sandy resigned himself to being their hot water bottle. Both Siamese made remarkable recoveries, and before long were fit and healthy specimens; so much so that Tigger had a parade of three admirers who regularly assembled in the garden. This barbershop trio became so plaintive that Tigger succumbed, and from her second litter came a grey and white kitten called Theo, who grew rapidly into a genial giant towering over the three delicate orientals.

Theo assumed TinTin's literary mantle and was soon hard at work writing a weekly column for the parish magazine. After a few issues of the feline column it became abundantly clear that Theo was not engaging the affections of her readers, and the column reverted to its previous author, an unassuming church mouse.

Whilst Theo was busy setting her thoughts to paper, the other three cats were busy making contributions to parish life at home: Pooh decided to enliven parish meetings by bringing in a selection of toys each week. These were generously distributed amongst those present, whilst Tigger and Sandy sang in discordant chorus outside the door. No wonder some of the parishioners are nervous about the cats' roles in parish life.

The cats' discordant chorus unnerved some parishioners.

Sandy still braves the North Sea breezes.

Acknowledgements

The author and publishers would like to thank the following
for their help and cooperation in making this book possible:

Rev. Dr Julian Scharf, All Saints', West Ham

Father Neil Hook, St John's, Brecon

Rev. Anthony and Mrs Anne Wintle, St Fagan's, Cardiff

Alan and Judy Lloyd, and the Rev. Dr Colin Beevers, St Michael and All Saints', Ledbury

Brother Aidan and the Franciscan Friars, Hilfield Friary

Patrick and Katherine Williams-Dienes, Norwich Cathedral

Judith Coles and Tessa Hoyes, St Mary's, Little Birch

Joanna and Susan Chorley, Tewkesbury Abbey

Rev. Brian and Mrs Tessa Curnew, Imogen Curnew, St Laurence's, Ludlow

Rev. Christopher and Mrs Christine Andrews, St Wulfram's, Grantham

Rev. Victor Stock, St Mary-le-Bow, London

Rev. Peter and Mrs Ruth Holliday, Holy Trinity, Stratford-upon-Avon

Rev. David and Mrs Christine Littlefair, Malmesbury Abbey

Rev. Charles and Mrs Gillian Townsend, St Peter and St Paul's, North Curry, Somerset

Rev. David and Mrs Christine Reynolds, St Wilfrid's Brayton, Selby

Canon Francis and Mrs Brenda Hewitt, St Peter and St Paul's, Pickering

Brother Joseph and the Benedictine community, Buckfast Abbey

Canon Murray and Mrs Deborah Haig, St Michael's, Alnwick